I CAN PLAY TOO!

In addition to *I Can Play Too!* We are delighted to offer several other titles from Solid Ground Christian Books for the young. Here are many of them:

Little Pillows and Morning Bells by Francis Havergal
Morning Stars by Francis Havergal
The Child's Book on the Fall by Thomas H. Gallaudet
The Child's Book on the Soul by Thomas H. Gallaudet
The Child's Book of Natural Theology by Thomas H. Gallaudet
The Child's Book on the Sabbath by Horace Hooker
Scripture Biography for the Young: Adam – Judges by Thomas H. Gallaudet
The Child's Preacher by Alexander Fletcher & J.C. Ryle
Feed My Lambs by John Todd
Truth Made Simple by John Todd
Nuts for Boys to Crack by John Todd
The Tract Primer by the American Tract Society
The Child at Home by John S.C. Abbott
Early Piety Illustrated by Gorham Abbott
Repentance & Faith for the Young by Charles Walker
Jesus the Way by Edward Payson Hammond
The Pastor's Daughter by Louisa Payson Hopkins
Lectures on the Bible to the Young by John Eadie
The Scripture Guide by James W. Alexander
My Brother's Keeper by James W. Alexander
The Chief End of Man by John Hall
Old Paths for Little Feet by Carol Brandt
Small Talks on Big Questions by Selah Helms & Susan Thompson Kahler
Advice to a Young Christian by Jared Waterbury
Bible Promises by Richard Newton
Bible Warnings by Richard Newton
Bible Models by Richard Newton
Bible Animals by Richard Newton
Bible Jewels by Richard Newton
Heroes of the Early Church by Richard Newton
Heroes of the Reformation by Richard Newton
Leaves from the Tree of Life by Richard Newton
Pebbles from the Brook by Richard Newton
Safe Compass and How it Points by Richard Newton
The King's Highway by Richard Newton
The Life of Jesus Christ for the Young by Richard Newton
Rays from the Sun of Righteousness by Richard Newton

Call us at 205-443-0311
Visit us on-line at www.solid-ground-books.com or write us an email at mike.sgcb@gmail.com

I CAN PLAY TOO!

Life-Changing Lessons from a Three-Legged Dog

SHARMAN MARTIN

Photographs by Karim Shamsi-Basha

Solid Ground Christian Books
Birmingham, Alabama USA

Solid Ground Christian Books
PO Box 660132
Vestavia Hills AL 35266
205-443-0311
mike.sgcb@gmail.com
www.solid-ground-books.com

I CAN PLAY TOO!
Life-Changing Lessons from a Three-Legged Dog
By Sharman Martin

Photography by Sharman Martin and Karim Shamsi-Basha

Cover and book design by Borgo Publishing
Contact them at borgogirl@bellsouth.net

Contact Karim Shamsi-Basha at karimshamsibasha@gmail.com

Paperback ISBN- 978-159925-343-5
Hardcover ISBN- 978-159925-344-2

I dedicate this book to my friend, Dawn Norris. Dawn is a friend and co-worker and she saw the diamond in the rough when I emailed her the draft I had written of *I Can Play Too!*. Dawn is the guidance counselor at Vestavia Hills Elementary School-West, the school where we both teach and she immediately knew that she wanted to use Bo's story/my book, as a lesson on Acceptance with every class in our K-3 school. She also scheduled dates for the children to meet Bo. As if that wasn't enough, Dawn contacted a local news station and was instrumental in getting Bo's story aired on a special called *The Spirit of Alabama*. Had it not been for Dawn's lesson with the children, and the impact it had on each of them, I probably wouldn't have persevered in pursuing the book's publication. Thank you Dawn for loving Boskee! We love you!

*"For God sees not as man sees,
for man looks at the outward appearance,
but the Lord looks at the heart."*

1 SAMUEL 16:7

ACKNOWLEDGMENTS

There are many people to thank for supporting my journey as I wrote this book, but I suppose I need to start at the top. I thank God for the animals He has created and especially for my three dogs. And I especially thank Him for sending Bo to me. A special thank you to my family whose support has always been insurmountable. I have been blessed with so many friends throughout my life that to name each one would take several pages and I would be devastated if anyone was left out. So a huge thank you to every friend in my life who has supported my love for writing.

The view from my back deck is breathtaking. It's especially beautiful as the sun is setting just behind the trees and the sky is illuminated with an orange-colored hue. My deck and backyard overlook a pasture complete with a creek, a winding country road, and winsome trees. On the other side of the pasture there use to live a three-legged yellow lab named Bo. I first saw Bo about three years ago when my two barking dogs drew my attention to the barn. I saw a handsome dog and noticed immediately that he had a very visible limp. I initially thought he was injured in some way but quickly discovered that he only had three legs.

Bo lost his leg as the result of stepping into a beaver trap. His previous owner told me that Bo had been missing for about a week and when they found him, he was lying in the creek. I was told had he not stayed in the creek, he would have bled out. The cold water stopped the bleeding. Even though gangrene had set in and amputating his leg was inevitable, by the grace of God, Bo survived this horrible accident.

Fast forward to New Year's Eve one year ago when I came home and discovered Bo in my garage. Like most dogs, Bo is terrified of fireworks and he found his way to my house after being frightened. I immediately saw something special in this dog. He rambled up to me and collapsed at my feet, pleading for

me to pet him. After a few moments of some well needed and deserved attention, I bedded Bo down for the evening and called his owner the following morning. Bo was retrieved a little while later and taken back home. I'll admit that even after such a brief encounter with Bo that night, I felt sad when he was taken back home.

Then in May 2013, Bo came back to see me…several times! Within a month, Bo journeyed to my house a minimum of ten times. With every call to Bo's owner that I made, the harder it was to make that call. Each time he came to see me, he stole a little more of my heart and in the back of my mind I was trying to convince myself that I could financially afford three dogs. Some days, I would wait a day or so before I'd call Bo's owner, just so I could have a little extra time with him. I knew that his owner knew where he was and if he wanted him, he'd come and get him… eventually. It's important to understand the distance of Bo's journey because his house isn't even visible from mine. I have estimated his journey to be about 200 yards from his house to mine. And this dog made that trip over and over and over again. Every time he reached my house he'd be wet and dirty and several times I'd pull ticks off of him. I gave him several baths, which secretly I think he loved! Bo completely stole my heart when he came over one Friday morning and stayed until Tuesday evening. When the truck pulled out of the driveway that Tuesday evening, with Bo in the back of it, I cried. I didn't have to cry for long though because two days later, he was back! I came home from school and he was in the garage waiting for me. I loved on him and checked him for ticks and was absolutely elated that he was back. Then I caved, and called his owner. It didn't feel right because I knew Bo wasn't mine to keep. His owner came and got him and the water works really started this time. Right then I decided that if Bo came back to me again, I'd ask if I could keep him. A week passed and no Bo. No matter what I did, I couldn't stop thinking about Bo and I'd look for him everyday when I came home from work.

One evening as I was sitting on my deck, I spontaneously got on my knees and prayed for Bo to come back. I knew this dog was special and that he and I belonged together. Then one Monday night I heard the dogs barking. I jumped up, grabbed a flashlight and ran outside to see if it could possibly be Bo. I shined the light towards the pasture and even though Bo hadn't come into vision yet, I could hear his recognizable shuffle through the tall grass. I remember smiling from ear to ear as I ran down the steps to meet him at the fence. We had some joyful hugging and kissing time, even though he smelled like a dirty wet dog! Once again I bedded Bo down for the night on my front porch with blankets and pillows. I was afraid to bring him inside until he was completely flea and tick free. The following morning, I heard his owner pull in to my driveway. I met him on the front porch and asked the question that I prayed would follow with a "yes" answer. His owner told me that he needed to think about it and would let me know in a few days. He left Bo with me during that time. I really got the prayer warriors going after that conversation. Some may think praying for a dog to become a member of one's household is silly, and maybe it is, but I prayed anyway! I received an email that following Friday from Bo's owner, and as they say, the rest is history. I immediately took him to my Veterinarian and she treated Bo for fleas and ticks, gave him a complete once over and other than only having three legs, he was given a clean bill of health.

Looking back on the order of events that brought Bo into my life, I realize that God isn't so busy that he can't help us with all our needs—big and small. He directed Bo to me, just like He directed him to the creek years back. He is guiding both of us as we share our story about acceptance and treating others with kindness. I try not to think about the fact that Bo is 13 years old…it makes me sad. However, I know that God started my incredible journey with Bo and He will see it through to the end.

I know I look different than all the rest

But that doesn't mean I feel second best.

I can do the things that most dogs do...

Run, jump, swim, and chew!

I have two brothers, I think they're the best!

But they don't like me 'cause
I look different than the rest.

So I watch them wrestle, jump, and play.

And wish so badly they'd look my way.

My little brother, he's coming around...

He's the cutest of all hounds!

He doesn't snarl. growl, or snap

When I try to lie down on my owner's lap.

But the big one, well...let's just say,

I think he'd love it if I just went away.

I want to tell him, "I can play too!"

"Just give me a chance to prove it to you!"

"It's because you look different,"
whispers little brother to me.

"I know, I know...all he sees is three."

Three legs that is, instead of four.

"If he'd play with me just once, he'd love me for sure!"

Patiently I wait, in hopes of getting to play,

As I watch them have fun day after day.

I guess I'm just different, and won't ever be the same,

As I watch my brothers running
and playing their fun games.

Then one day clear out of the blue,

They started playing and wanted me to play too!

"Thanks little brother for helping him see,

that it's okay for him to play with me."

"No problem," said little brother
as he grinned and winked.

And I knew then that he'd helped
my big brother to think...

to think about not making me feel ashamed.

Because we're all dogs, we're all just the same.

ALL THINGS BRIGHT AND BEAUTIFUL

All things bright and beautiful,
All creatures great and small,
All things wise and wonderful,
The Lord God made them all.

Each little flower that opens,
Each little bird that sings,
He made their glowing colors,
He made their tiny wings.
The tall trees in the greenwood,
The meadows where we play,
The rushes by the water,
We gather every day;–

He gave us eyes to see them,
And lips that we might tell,
How great is God Almighty,
Who has made all things well.
All things bright and beautiful,
All creatures great and small,
All things wise and wonderful,
The Lord God made them all.

—WORDS BY CECIL FRANCES ALEXANDER

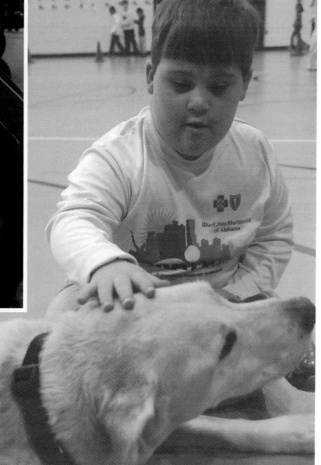

Bo's Special Friends: Lonnie Smith, Noah Bryant and Jaiden Davis.

Coming Summer 2014

Bo Meets A Hero is Martin's second book. The book features a special Iraq Veteran, Noah Galloway, United States Army, 101st Airborne Division (Air Assault). Noah and Bo become friends and bond as they realize that their lives aren't over due to their physical changes—it just becomes a different life than what they both once knew.

Sharman Martin graduated from The University of West Florida with a Bachelor's Degree in Early Childhood/ Elementary Education. She has taught 1st grade, 3rd grade, and is presently teaching Elementary Physical Education at Vestavia West Elementary School in Vestavia Hills, Alabama. She is a veteran teacher of 24 years. Sharman lives in rural McCalla, Alabama with her 3 dogs, Aubie, Opie, and Bo. She enjoys reading true crime and mystery novels, spending time with family and friends, and spoiling her dogs as much as possible. Writing has always been her passion and Sharman has finally seen her dream come true with the publication of *I Can Play Too*.

Karim Shamsi-Basha

is an award-winning writer and photographer. He was born in Damascus, Syria in 1965, and immigrated to the United States in 1984. He is fluent in both Arabic and English. His work as a photojournalist has been published in magazines all over the world including: *National Geographic Traveler, Sports Illustrated, People, Time, Southern Living, Coastal Living, The New York Times, The Washington Post,* and *Parenting* just to name a few. He has traveled on assignments to countries including: China, France, the Czech Republic, Mexico, Turkey, Italy, and Chile. He is blessed with three precious children: Zade, Dury and Demi. Karim's autobiography titled *PAUL and Me* was published in 2013 by Solid Ground.

"I am Bo....I am loved."

CPSIA information can be obtained
at www.ICGtesting.com
Printed in the USA
LVIC04n0034060514
384538LV00001B/1